Valen Day Jokes for Kids

A Valentine's Day Book for Children

Plus 5 Bonus Activities!

by Chrissy Voeg

PHILADELPHIA PA

Chrissy Voeg

Philadelphia PA

ISBN 978-1542365390

Printed in the United States of America

Valentine's Day Jokes

Q: What did the boy octopus say to the girl octopus?

A: I want to hold your hand, hand, hand, hand, hand, hand, hand, hand.

Q: What kind of flower is bad to give on valentines' day?

A: Cauliflower!

Knock Knock

Who's there?

Ima

Ima who?

Ima hoping I get lots of cards on Valentine's Day!

Knock Knock

Who's there?

Luke

Luke who?

Luke who got a Valentine!

Chrissy Voeg

Q: What did the stamp say to the envelope?

A: I'm stuck on you.

Q: What did the envelope say back to the stamp?

A: Stick with me and we'll go places!

Q: Why did the boy put candy under his pillow?

A: Because he wanted sweet dreams!

Q: What do bunnies do when they get married?

A: They go on a bunnymoon!

Q. What did the girl say when the by asked if she had a date for Valentine's Day?

A. She said "Of course, it is February 14th!"

Q: What did the monster say to the other monster?

A: Will you be my Valen-slime?

Q: What do farmers give their wives on Valentine's Day?

A: Hogs and kisses!

Q: What did the chocolate syrup say to the ice cream on Valentine's Day?

A: I'm sweet on you.

Q: What did the blueberry say to her sweetie on Valentine's Day?

A: I love you berry much.

Q. What did one volcano say to the other on Valentine's Day?

A. I lava you.

Q: What did the painter say to his girlfriend on Valentine's Day?

A: I love you with all of my art!

Q: What did one sheep say to the other sheep on Valentine's Day?

A: I love ewe.

Q: What did the sheep say in return?

A: I love you baaaaaaaaaack.

Q: Why did they put the boy's girlfriend in jail?

A: Because she stole his heart.

Q: What did the owl say to the other owl on Valentine's Day?

A: Owl always be yours.

Q: What did the boy bee say to the girl bee on Valentine's Day?

A: You are bee-utiful, honey.

Q: What did the bear say to his sweetie on Valentine's Day?

A: I love you bear-y much.

Q: Why did the cats get married?

A: Because they are purrr-fect for each other.

Q: What do you call two birds in love?

A: Tweet-hearts.

Q: What did one oar say to the other?

A: Can I interest you in a little row-mance?

Q: What did the paper clip say to the magnet?

A: I find you very attractive.

Q: What is it called when fish fall in love?

A: Guppy-love!

Q: Why did the pig give his girlfriend a box of candy?

A: It was Valen-swine's Day.

Q: What do you call a very small Valentine?

A: A valen-tiny.

Q: Why shouldn't you break up with a goalie?

A: Because she's a keeper.

Q: Do skunks celebrate Valentine's Day?

A: Yes, they are very scent-imental!

Q: How did the telephone propose to his girlfriend?

A: He gave her a ring.

Q: What did one piece of string say to the other?

A: Will you be my Valen-twine?

Q: What do squirrels give for Valentine's Day?

A: Forget-me-nuts!

Chrissy Voeg

Knock Knock.

Who's there?

Olive.

Olive who?

Olive you!

Knock Knock.

Who's there?

Sherwood.

Sherwood who?

Sherwood like to be your valentine.

Q: What did the bat say to his girlfriend on Valentine's Day?

A: I love hanging out with you!

Chrissy Voeg

Q: What did Pilgrims give each other on Valentine's Day?

A: Mayflowers

Q: What did the rabbit say to his girlfriend on Valentine's Day?

A: Somebunny loves you.

Q: What did the elephant say to her husband on Valentine's Day?

A: I love you a ton.

Q: What did one calculator say to the other on Valentine's Day?

A: Let me count the ways I love you.

Q: What question does Frankenstein ask on Valentine's Day?

A: Where is my Valen-stein?

Q: What did one snake say to the other snake?

A: Give me a hiss, honey.

Q: Why did the banana go out with the prune?

A: Because it couldn't get a date.

Q. Did Adam and Eve ever have a date?

A. No, but they had an apple.

Q: What did the drum say to the other drum on Valentine's Day?

A: My heart beats for you.

Knock Knock.

Who's there?

Frank.

Frank who?

Frank you for being my friend!

Knock Knock.

Who's there?

Howard.

Howard who?

Howard you like a big Valentine's Day kiss?

Q: What does one ghost say to another on Valentine's Day?

A: I love boo!

Q: What is a vampire's sweetheart called?

A: His ghoul-friend.

Q. What did the husband ghost say to his wife?

A. You are so boo-tiful!

Q: Why did the light bulb say to her boyfriend?

A: I love you a watt!

Knock Knock.

Who's there?

Arthur.

Arthur who?

Arthur any chocolates left for me?

Knock Knock.

Who's there?

Pooch

Pooch who?

Pooch your arms around me, baby!

Chrissy Voeg

Q: Why did the rooster cross the road?

A: He wanted to impress the chicks!

Q: What is a deer's favorite song?

A: I only have eyes for you, deer.

Q: If your aunt runs off to get married, what would you call her?

A: Ant-elope!

Q: What did the French chef give his wife for Valentine's Day?

A: Hugs and quiches.

Q: Why did the cannibal break up with his girlfriend?

A: She didn't suit his taste!

Q: What did the caveman give his wife on Valentine's day?

A: Kisses and ughs!

Q: When the boy squirrel said "I'm nuts about you" to the girl squirrel, what did she say back?

A: "You're nuts so bad yourself!"

Q: What do single people say to each other on Valentine's Day?

A: Happy Independence Day!

Valentine's Day Activities

Chrissy Voeg

Who is Your Valentine?

Who is special to you on this Valentine's Day. Draw the person or people (or pets!) below.

Chrissy Voeg

Valentine's Day Match-Up

Valentines Day is celebrated in 6 countries. Can you match the countries with their names?

United States   Mexico   Canada

United Kingdom   France   Australia

Chrissy Voeg

Heart Designs

Which of the hearts below is your favorite?
What colors would you color them?

Chrissy Voeg

History of Valentines Day

Hundreds of years ago, people started giving each other handwritten notes or other small tokens of affection for Valentine's Day. In what century do you think this practice started?

1600s   1700s   1800s   1900s

Chrissy Voeg

Valentine's Day Maze

Can you find the way from start to finish?

Made in the USA
Middletown, DE
08 February 2020